geography on display

JOURNEY MAP

CAN YOU SPOT THE RIVER FEATURES?

MEANDERS

TRIBUTARIES

SOURCE

WATERFALL

FLOOD PLAIN

Claire Tinker

Acknowledgements

The author and publisher would like to thank the children from Hunter's Bar and Nook Lane Junior Schools for their amazing enthusiasm and talent in producing the artwork for this book. Thanks are also due to the many staff for their interest, advice, geographical help and hard work, especially to Gina and Mary for their encouragement and total commitment to art and design in the primary school.

Claire Tinker would also like to thank all her family and friends for putting up with her creative isolation and supporting her passion for all things 'arty'. A special thank you goes to daughters Liz, Amanda and particularly Celina for all their help, and the biggest thank you of all to husband Ian for his support and encouragement during the making of this book.

Taj Mahal Pictures (page 14)

First published in 2005 by Belair Publications.
Apex Business Centre, Boscombe Road, Dunstable, LU5 4RL.

Commissioning Editor: Zoë Nichols   Editor: Jill Adam
Page Layout: Suzanne Ward   Photography: RB Photography
Cover Design: Steve West

© 2005 Folens on behalf of the author.

Every effort has been made to trace the copyright holders of material used in this publication. If any copyright holder has been overlooked, we should be pleased to make the necessary arrangements.

British Library Cataloguing in Publication Data. A catalogue record for this publication is available from the British Library.

ISBN 094788 280 4

Contents

Introduction

The language of art will always hold an enthusiastic excitement for children and promoting creativity is a powerful and successful way of engaging children with their learning. Quite simply, children enjoy art. It is hard to separate one part of the curriculum from another so what better way is there to help develop skills and understanding, and provide enjoyment in lots of different areas, than through art?

The geography curriculum is rich in opportunities for creativity, which is widely acknowledged to help raise children's self-esteem and develop valuable skills for adult life. The world around us is an accessible, fascinating resource for exploring and developing ideas and exciting the imagination of the children in our care. The aim of this book is to celebrate children's entitlement to a rich, broad and balanced set of learning experiences linking the primary art and geography curricula. It is arranged into 14 sections, each with a different geographical focus, suitable across the age groups, 5–11. The various themes provide opportunities for responding to natural and made objects and environments. There are activities, where the work of artists from different periods and cultures is investigated, that use a variety of materials and processes in both 2-D and 3-D.

Each theme begins with a visual geographical starting point and is then developed through several linked art ideas. Since the delivery of the geography scheme is fairly flexible and not always confined to prescriptive age groups, the work has been produced by children of various ages to demonstrate how the themes can be dipped into or adapted to suit the required year group.

Displaying children's work imaginatively makes a distinctive contribution to the aesthetic environment of the school. Well-thought-out displays not only provide interactive learning opportunities but value children's achievements and relay an impressive message to all visitors to the school. The displays in this book attempt to further children's understanding of the world around them, making it vivid and real, and celebrating their response to it. I hope it provides ideas and inspires further cross-curricular creativity and enjoyment.

Claire Tinker

Through My Window

Take photographs somewhere in your locality where the skyline is clearly visible. Discuss how much information photographs can give about the character of a place. Ask the children what human activities have created this view and how it might have looked before human intervention. What features of the area, in terms of land use and function, are visible in the pictures? Consider how a photograph taken from another point in the area would show different features.

Resources
- Camera
- *Window* by Jeannie Baker (Walker Books)
- Large piece of fabric
- Orange fabric dye
- Collage materials
- Card and glue
- Curtain fabric

Approach

1. Show the children the collage pictures in Jeannie Baker's book *Window* (published by Walker Books). Explain that you are going to create a large collage of your local area in the same style.

2. Tie and dye a large piece of cloth orange for the background.

3. Refer to the original photographs of your area and discuss what features need to be shown on the collage.

4. Talk about the scale of buildings and explain that those nearest will be larger than the ones on the skyline. Provide a variety of collage materials. Allocate a particular area of the collage for each child or group to work on.

5. Bring all the elements of the view together on the fabric background and stick them down firmly, starting at the skyline and working towards the front of the collage.

6. Display in the style of Jeannie Baker's book, with a person looking at the view through a window. Add a card window frame and some curtains.

Photographic Collage

In the 1980s British artist, David Hockney (born 1937) experimented with photography to create a series of photographic collages. These landscape collages give a wider perspective to the viewer than conventional photography. The prints can be arranged to create movement. The results of recreating a familiar local scene in this style can be a powerful way to make the onlooker feel as if they are in the picture with the scene all around them.

Approach

Resources
- Camera
- Card
- Glue

1. Take several photographs of a view that is familiar to the children. If possible provide groups of children with a camera to take the photographs themselves, choosing the scene carefully.

2. Explain that the photographs have to include the whole view so they should stand in one place and move the camera around in a semi-circle (between shots!) in order to take photographs that are close together.

3. Have duplicates of each photograph printed to enable greater scope for cutting and sticking all the different areas.

4. Ask the groups to lay out their photographs on a sheet of card to recreate the scene of their choice.

5. Encourage the children to cut photographs if necessary, then to stick down firmly when all the prints are in position.

Recycling Posters

The emphasis on the world of advertising and consumerism in the pop art movement makes this an ideal source of inspiration for posters on recycling.

Resources
● Pop art posters
● Bottles and/or tin cans
● Paints and paintbrushes
● Paper or card and glue

Approach

1. Discuss what people do with their rubbish locally. What are the methods of re-using and recycling waste in the local area? Set the children a homework task to research what is available.

2. Collect evidence of litter and environmental damage around the school and consider ways of improving the affected areas in the buildings and grounds.

3. Talk about how the actions of individuals on a local level can make a difference to global environmental problems.

4. Look at the pop art work of American artist Andy Warhol (1928–1987). Adapt his ideas to design a poster advertising a bottle bank or tin can recycling depot.

5. Ask the children to work in groups, observing bottles or cans and making careful paintings of them.

6. Type the title and recycling messages. Stick the paintings of bottles or cans around the message to create a pop art poster.

7

Sky Moods

The choice of sky colour in pictures dramatically affects the composition and mood of a landscape. Look at some pictures or photographs of sunsets with the children and discuss the mixtures of colours.

Resources
- Pictures or photographs of sunset landscapes
- Photocopies of a black and white photograph of local rooftops
- White paper and glue
- Chalk pastels

Approach

1. Cut off and discard the sky area from the photocopied picture of local rooftops. Ask each child to stick the copy onto a large sheet of white paper.

2. Discuss where the photograph was taken. Ask the children to guess what time of day and in which season it was taken.

3. Explain how difficult it is to answer these questions without the clues that the sky provides. Look again at the range of pictures of landscapes with different skies. Ask questions about the time of day and discuss the importance of the sky for setting the mood of the picture.

4. Ask the children to choose a mood they want to create. Discuss the possibilities, from menacing thunderstorms to clear blue skies on a summer's day. Emphasise that the sky can be many different colours – red, purple, green, blue, black, grey, yellow – all will give a different atmosphere.

5. Use chalk pastels to colour the sky.

6. Compare how the different skies make us feel. Which compositions make us feel relaxed and restful? Which pictures create a feeling of unease?

Beauty Spot Mural

Resources
- Photographs of local beauty spots
- Cartridge paper
- Paints and paintbrushes
- Glue

Approach

1. Take a photograph of a local beauty spot and divide it up into the same number of rectangles as pupils working on the activity. Before cutting it up, number the rectangles on the back so they can easily be reconstructed when the mural is put together.

2. Give each child a rectangle of the photograph and some paper. Ask them to copy down the number of their piece of photograph onto the back of their paper

3. Ask the children to recreate their rectangle of the photograph as carefully and realistically as possible, with paints, working right to the edges of the paper.

4. Join the painted sections together to create a group mural of the local beauty spot.

5. For another activity, give each child a piece of the scene photographed. Stick it onto the centre of a piece of cartridge paper and ask them to extend the colours and shapes to fill the paper.

6. In both activities encourage the children to mix colours to recreate the exact shade of flowers and the landscape.

Research Project

Use globes and atlases to locate India. Talk about the scale of the country by comparing it to your own country. Look at pictures of the huge range of landscapes, from deserts and tropical jungles to the highest mountain in the world. India's climate is governed by the monsoon and most of the country has three seasons. Ask the children to find out what they are. Discuss the diversity and richness of Indian life and culture.

Resources
- Atlases
- Globes
- Pictures of Indian landscapes
- Card

Approach

1. Cut out the five letters of INDIA, in large format, from card.

2. Divide the class into five groups and brainstorm possible areas for research. These could include: wildlife of India; map of India with locations of cities, mountains and other features plotted; tourist attractions; religion and festivals in India.

3. Give each group a letter and an area of research. Challenge the children to find out as much as possible about their particular aspect of India using non-fiction books, encyclopedias and computers.

4. Ask the children to present their information visually on their group's letter. These images could start off fairly simply and be supplemented as the topic progresses.

5. When the topic is complete ask each group to present their letter to the rest of the class, backing up the visual image with written facts and information.

6. Display the letters to spell out the word INDIA.

Papier-mâché Elephants

In India, elephants are seen as strong and mighty beasts. At one time people believed that above the earth heavenly elephants held up the sky. In New Delhi on Republic Day (26th January) there is a national parade with elephants dressed in ornate fabrics and brightly coloured adornments.

Resources
- Balloons
- Cellulose paste powder and water
- Scrap paper
- Egg boxes
- Paints and paintbrushes
- Decorative collage materials
- Glue

Approach

1. Blow up a balloon and cover it with papier-mâché. Allow to dry.

2. Cut up cardboard egg boxes to use as feet and glue in place.

3. Scrunch up some paper to form the elephant's trunk. Glue in place.

4. Cut out two paper ears and stick to the body.

5. Cover the whole elephant in at least two layers of papier-mâché. Allow to dry.

6. Look at pictures of Indian elephants in their ceremonial dress. Ask the children to sketch out their own designs.

7. Paint the elephant and allow to dry. Add collage materials to make the elephant as decorative and eye-catching as possible.

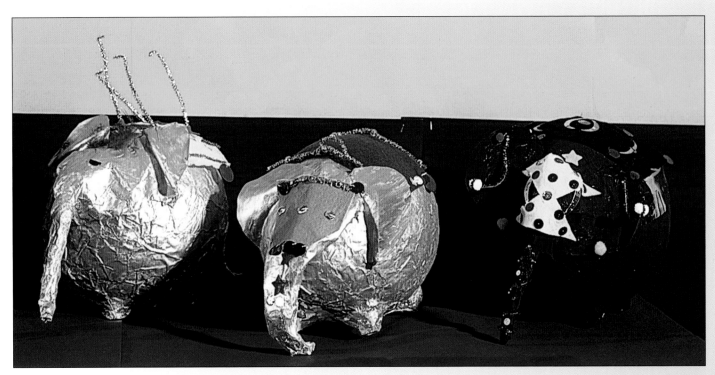

Mendhi-patterned Peacock

In India many textile patterns have been inspired by the peacock's brilliant plumage. Peacocks were often kept in gardens where, as well as adding to the beauty of the surroundings, they were used to ward off snakes. Mendhi designs are intricate patterns drawn on women's hands at festivals and celebrations. The designs are painted in henna and the deep red-brown colour can last for a couple of weeks.

Approach

1. Draw a large outline of a peacock on a piece of card and cover it with cardboard egg trays. Paint the egg trays in bright colours and glue on sequins to decorate.

2. For the peacock's feathers, ask the children to draw around their hands on thin card and cut out the shapes.

3. Using thin paintbrushes and matchsticks dipped in paint, decorate the card hands in detailed Mendhi patterns.

4. Display the hands around the peacock's body to represent its beautiful plumage.

Resources
- Card
- Matchsticks
- Paints and paintbrushes
- Cardboard egg trays
- Sequins and glue
- Examples of Mendhi patterns

Tie and Dye Cloth

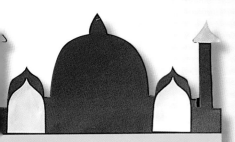

People in India have been weaving and decorating cloth for thousands of years. The Indian methods of tie-dying cloth are distinctive and fabrics are often covered with hundreds of tiny circles of colour.

Approach

1. Give each child a cotton square. To create a circular pattern place some dried peas or marbles on the fabric and secure in place by twisting elastic bands around them. Encourage the children to twist the bands as tightly as they can to stop the dye reaching this part of the cloth.

2. To create striped tie and dye patterns fold the fabric in a pleated fashion. Twist elastic bands around the folded cloth in several places.

3. Fill a bucket with cold water and stir in the powdered dye.

4. Place all the cotton squares into the dye, ensuring they are completely covered with the solution, and leave for an hour or so.

Resources
- Squares of cotton fabric
- Cold water dyes
- Bucket
- Elastic bands
- Dried peas or marbles
- Beads, sequins, felt, glittery pipe cleaners
- Iron

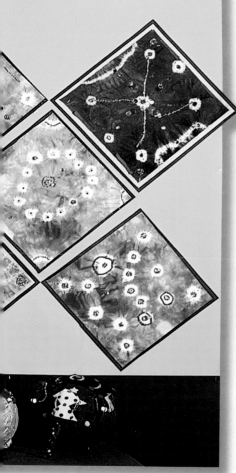

5. Remove the dyed squares, rinse them and leave to dry.

6. When dry, untie the squares and iron them.

7. Add felt patterns, sequins, beads and glittery pipe cleaners to embellish the designs.

⚠ **Note: An adult should use the iron at all times.**

Taj Mahal Pictures

The white marble Taj Mahal at Agra is one of the world's most famous sights. It was built in 1632 by the Mogul Emperor Shah Jahan as a tomb for his beloved wife, Mumtaz Mahal. Look at pictures of the Taj Mahal with the children and discuss its form and colours.

Approach

1. Give each child a serviette and sheet of white paper roughly the same size. Place the white serviette on top of the sheet of paper.

2. Using neat inks, paint a pattern onto the serviette. The inks will naturally seep into each other creating some lovely coloured effects.

3. Stress to the children that once wet the serviettes will become fragile. Once they start to paint, they should not try to remove them from the backing sheet.

4. Leave the serviettes to dry.

5. Look again at a picture of the Taj Mahal. Emphasise its symmetry to the children and ask them to draw it as carefully as they can on a sheet of thin, black card.

6. Cut out the picture and enhance some of the towers and domes in gold paint.

7. Stick the pictures of the Taj Mahal onto the dried serviette background.

8. Some will naturally lend themselves to being mounted in a circular shape while others will look better in rectangles. Display around a large simplified version of the Taj Mahal.

Resources
- White serviettes or napkins
- White paper
- Indian ink in bright sunset colours
- Black card or paper
- Gold paint and paintbrushes
- Pictures of the Taj Mahal

Silk Painting

India is one of the top producers of cotton and silk in the world. Most regions of India have different ways of dyeing and decorating cloth. Silk is often used to make saris which are worn at weddings and other special ceremonies. Look at some examples of silk paintings with the children.

Approach

Resources
- Illustrations of silk paintings
- Silk fabric
- Card
- Silk paint and gutta
- Paintbrushes
- Masking tape
- Sequins

1. Research some traditional Indian designs such as Mendhi patterns and peacocks. Ask the children to sketch out some ideas and discuss possible colours.

2. On a piece of card draw a design or picture, pressing hard with the pencil so the design will show through the silk fabric.

3. Place the silk on top of the design and tape around the edges.

4. Trace around the lines of the drawing in gutta, making sure that the gutta completely encloses areas of the silk.

5. Paint the design with silk paints and leave to dry.

6. Gently peel off the silk from the cardboard and mount it on a new piece of card.

7. The design left on the original card makes an interesting textured print and can be displayed alongside the silk pattern.

8. Give the children the chance to enhance the textures of both the silk and card designs by adding sequins or other decorative items.

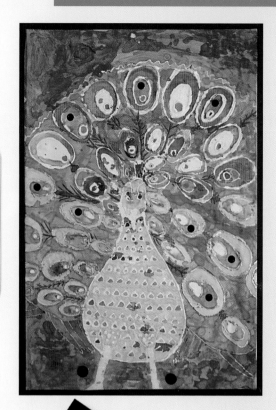

Folding Screen

Locate Japan on a world map and relate its position to your own country. Talk about possible ways of going to Japan. How far away is it? How long would it take to get there? Look at books, pictures and other resource material and talk about what there is to see and do in Japan.

Approach

1. Explain to the children that large paintings on folding screens have been used to decorate houses in Japan for many hundreds of years. The style of the screens is often extravagant, with rich colours and gold decorations. The subjects depicted include most aspects of nature.

2. Use the idea of a Japanese screen to portray elements of Japan. Brainstorm possible areas the children would like to explore, for example, Japanese clothes, food, houses and writing.

3. Fold a large, rectangular piece of paper into three sections. Glue sticks on the folds and at each end of the screen.

4. Guide the children in their research, and use one side of the screen to display appropriate artwork.

5. As the topic progresses and the children learn more about the country, encourage them to use the reverse side of the screen as a developing visual storyboard about life in Japan.

Resources
- Atlases
- Reference books on Japan
- Cartridge paper
- Wooden sticks and glue
- Art materials

Irises and Stream, Japanese Screen © Christie's Images/CORBIS

Japanese Kites

Kite-flying is a traditional art of great skill in Japan. Kite festivals are held during April and May. Some of the largest kites need teams of 20 people to fly them. The kites may measure up to 12 metres long and weigh as much as 40kg.

Approach

1. Observe Japanese kites, looking closely at the use of colour, decoration and pattern.

2. Talk to the children about collecting ideas from several different sources and designing their own kites.

3. Cut out large kite shapes from cartridge paper. Ask the children to design their own kite within these shapes.

4. Paint the kites and embellish them with tissue or crêpe paper.

Resources
- Cartridge paper
- Paints and paintbrushes
- Pictures of Japanese kites
- Tissue or crêpe paper
- Glue

Lacquered Boxes

Lacquer is a hard, waterproof resin that comes from the sap of the lacquer tree. It has been used in Japan for hundreds of years to decorate objects and give them a glossy appearance. One particular technique of lacquering is to inlay or sprinkle on tiny pieces of real gold while the lacquer is still wet.

Approach

1. If using a net, make up the boxes and leave to dry. Paint the boxes completely black.

2. Use gold paint to decorate the boxes. Sprinkle on gold glitter while the paint is still wet.

3. When dry, varnish the boxes to give them a lacquered look.

Resources
- Ready-made boxes (or card and nets)
- Black and gold paint
- Gold glitter
- Varnish
- Paintbrushes

Japanese Lanterns

Thousands of people from across Japan go to Kyoto every July to celebrate the Gion Festival. There is a parade through the streets and paper lanterns are lit on the night before the procession to decorate the city.

Resources
- Brightly coloured paper
- Paints and paintbrushes
- Tissue paper
- Glue

Approach

1. Fold a rectangular piece of paper in half lengthways.

2. Cut at regular intervals through the folded paper from the folded edge to within a couple of centimetres of the cut edges.

3. Open up the paper, decorate with cut-out shapes and paint.

4. For extra strength, glue two strips of paper to the top and bottom of the lantern.

5. Glue or staple the paper to form a tubular lantern.

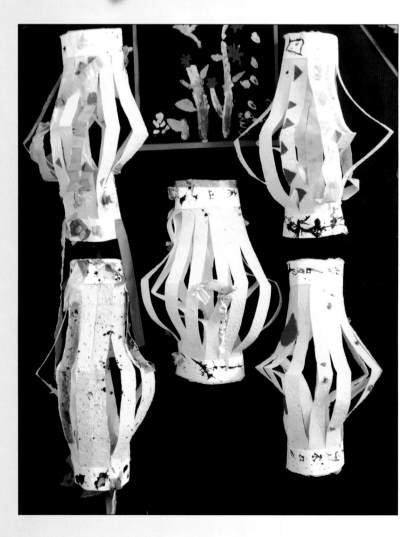

Japanese Fans

The folded fan was invented by the Japanese. Usually made out of silk or paper, they are decorated with ink or paint. Cherry blossom, the national flower of Japan, is often chosen as a decorative motif.

Approach

1. Give each child a strip of coloured paper.

2. Show the children pictures of Japanese fans. Point out the shapes and patterns and demonstrate how to copy them.

3. Ask the children to draw the patterns onto their strips of paper.

Resources
- Coloured paper
- Paints and paintbrushes
- Straws
- Pictures of Japanese fans

4. Paint the designs. Fine apple blossom can be created by blow-painting blobs of paint into twisted branches, with pink blossom painted on top.

5. Display all the decorated strips as one large circular fan, as shown.

Japanese Kimonos

The kimono is a traditional garment. In the past it was worn by men, women and children and made out of cotton or linen. Today kimonos are worn on special occasions. They are generally brightly coloured and embroidered for decoration.

Resources
- Card
- Black fabric
- Felt
- Paints and paintbrushes
- Glue
- Pictures of Japanese kimonos

Approach

1. For each child cut a kimono shape out of fabric and stick it onto card.

2. Show the children pictures of kimonos. Discuss the patterns and colours.

3. Ask the children to draw similar patterns on the fabric. Paint, and add appliqué felt flowers.

4. A sash could be made from a contrasting piece of fabric or paper.

Eye on Africa

The continent of Africa covers more than one fifth of the earth's land surface. It is made up of many different countries where more than 1000 different languages are spoken. Art is everywhere in Africa; a great richness and variety of images and designs – religious, historical, graphic and cultural – reflect aspects of African life. Talk about the different types of African art the children have already heard about. Research new ones from cave paintings, pottery, body art, textiles and metal. Discuss what each type of art tells us about the traditions, geography and history of Africa.

Approach

1. Give each child a map of Africa to trace and cut out in cartridge paper.

2. Using a variety of research material, sketch out on a separate piece of paper images of African life as depicted in different types of African art.

3. Transfer these images onto the map of Africa.

4. Display on a board covered in black paper, with a large pair of spectacles cut out of card. Inside the lenses of the spectacles could be a map of the world, placing Africa in context, or a picture of one aspect of African life or wildlife. As the topic progresses and the focus for research changes, so could the image through the lenses.

5. Encourage the children to look at each map and talk about what it tells us of African life.

Resources
- Map of Africa
- Reference books and materials
- Cartridge paper
- Black paper or board
- Card

Papier-mâché Ceramics

Contemporary African artists often use traditional images as inspiration for their work, but also adopt western styles and techniques to develop their ideas.

Resources
- Plates and bowls
- Petroleum jelly
- Cellulose paste powder and water
- Scrap paper
- Paints and paintbrushes
- Pictures of African art
- Viewfinders

Approach

1. Using different-sized plates and bowls as moulds, cover the top surfaces with a thin layer of petroleum jelly, then several layers of papier-mâché. When dry, remove the mould. Trim around the edges of the papier-mâché.

2. Look at some contemporary African artwork. Use a viewfinder to focus attention on a particular area, which uses colours and designs that appeal.

3. Refer to the area highlighted by the viewfinder to develop a contemporary design. Try it out on paper first, then paint the design onto the papier-mâché plates and bowls.

Collage Collars

Many African tribes-people traditionally wear some form of decorative necklace, headband or earrings. In the past these were made from glass beads imported into Africa by Italian merchants in the 16th century. Today they are made from plastic beads and can include recycled objects such as buttons and bottle tops. The designs and number of beaded necklaces worn by Masai women reflect the wealth and status of the wearer.

Resources
- Card
- Collage materials
- Glue
- Paint and paintbrushes

Approach

1. Cut out circular collars from card – one per child. Look at pictures of beadwork and sketch out some ideas on scrap paper.

2. Using collage materials such as beads, painted pasta and art straws, build up patterns onto the card and stick down firmly.

Animal Banners

Banners are often made in Africa to be carried at special ceremonies such as weddings. They are brightly coloured and enhanced with appliqué work. Many banners feature pictures of animals, insects and plants.

Resources
- Large sheets of thick calico – one per banner
- Fabric paints and paintbrushes
- Felt and other appliqué fabrics and glue

Approach

1. Working from African symbols and images, ask the children to sketch a design of an African animal on a coloured, patterned background. Stress the colours and shapes do not have to be purely representational and that just part of the animal can be portrayed.

2. With children in groups of three or four, ask them to choose one of the animal sketches to enlarge onto the calico. Combine several of the other children's background designs to create the banner.

3. Discuss colours and paint the cloth.

4. Explain that appliqué is the technique of sticking or sewing designs cut out of fabric onto a larger piece of cloth. Discuss which areas of the banner need enhancing. Cut out felt or fabric appliqué shapes to add to the banner.

5. Display with other pictures of African animals and large 'jungle' letters, spelling AFRICA.

Ostrich Egg Water Carriers

Ostrich racing is a popular spectator sport in parts of Africa. Empty ostrich eggshells make useful water carriers that may last for several years. The shells can be the same size as a melon and hold approximately a litre of water.

Resources
- Balloons
- Cellulose paper paste and water
- Scrap paper
- White paint
- Black paint or charcoal
- Paintbrushes

Approach

1. Blow up a balloon and paste several layers of torn scrap paper onto it. Cover the whole balloon and allow to dry.

2. Paint the papier-mâché white, then pop the balloon. Cut a small section from the top of the shell, large enough to get a hand inside.

3. Study designs of ostrich egg water carriers. These could be simple pictures of animals or people, drawn onto the shells, then rubbed over with charcoal to make the designs stand out.

4. In pencil draw a design on the shell. Carefully go over the drawing with black paint or charcoal.

Mexican Flag Display

Look at pictures and books about Mexico showing ancient temples, modern cities, deserts, jungles, volcanoes and beaches. Mexico is one of the 20 richest nations in the world but there are huge differences in the standard of living between the poor and the wealthy. Discuss reasons why this should be. Mexico City is the world's most polluted city. Scientists have predicted that it will be impossible for people to live and work there by 2020 because of pollution. Talk about what causes the pollution and possible solutions. Explore the reasons why 20 million people visit Mexico each year and the impact this has on the economy and environment. As a class, brainstorm ideas and themes to include in a display about Mexico to show the varied landscape, climate and contrasting features of this vast country.

Resources
- Display board
- Coloured paper – green, white and red
- Map of Mexico
- Green tissue paper
- Matchsticks
- Cardboard
- Paints and paintbrushes
- Feathers
- Glue

Approach

1. Divide a display board into three sections using coloured backing paper to match the Mexican flag. Green is for independence, white is for religion and red stands for unity.

2. Draw a large map of Mexico in green paper and attach it to the white middle section of the board.

3. Divide the class into small groups to research in more detail a particular aspect of Mexico. Suggested themes are as follows:

   Desert Draw saguaro cacti, which can grow over 12 metres tall. Add texture with tissue paper and matchsticks.

   Temples and pyramids Look at pictures of the pyramid El Castillo in the ancient Mayan city of Chichén Itzá. Use cardboard rectangles to create the pyramid, and matchsticks on the side to represent the 365 steps up to the temple at the top.

   Festivals Cut out large balloon shapes in paper. Decorate with brightly coloured designs.

   Jungle Look at pictures of parrots and butterflies found in the lush tropical rainforests in southern Mexico. Draw parrots onto card. Paint and embellish the birds with coloured feathers.

Volcano Model

Mexico has a huge range of landscapes within its borders, that can be divided into three main types: mountain ranges and plateaux, peninsulas and the coastal plains. The highest peak is Citlatepetl, part of a chain of volcanic mountains running across the south of the country.

Approach

1. Look at pictures of the volcanic mountains in southern Mexico. Study the shapes of the ranges and the colours. What is a volcano? What happens when it erupts?

2. Mould the wire mesh into the shape of a volcanic mountain.

3. Soak the strips of modroc in water for 3–4 seconds, then cover the wire mesh.

4. When it is dry, paint the volcano, possibly adding texture with scrunched-up tissue paper.

5. Glue red, yellow and orange pipe cleaners and foil into the top of the crater to show the effects of the volcano erupting.

Resources
- Wire mesh
- Modroc plaster bandages
- Paints and paintbrushes
- Tissue paper (optional)
- Glue
- Pipe cleaners and aluminium foil

Mexican Mural

Hundreds of years ago the Maya painted elaborate, colourful murals showing scenes of wealthy people enjoying life. The tradition of wall painting is still popular, but modern murals present very different social themes, such as poverty and suffering. One of modern Mexico's most famous artists was Diego Rivera (1886–1957). Read *For Every Child* (published by Red Fox) with the class. In 1989 54 principles were adopted as the UN Convention on the Rights of the Child. *For Every Child*, produced in conjunction with UNICEF, is a picture book, concentrating on the 14 principles most relevant to young children. Discuss some of the issues affecting children in Mexico. More than half of all Mexicans are poor and many children have to work to earn money for their families. Explore the differences between the way some children in Mexico live and your pupils' own lives.

Approach

1. Look at the work of some Mexican mural painters and try to interpret the social injustice or human suffering they portray.

2. Ask each child to sketch out a picture based on a couple of human rights issues, for example, a child's right to education.

3. Paint pictures and transfer them onto the card and display as shown.

Resources
- *For Every Child* (Red Fox)
- Large sheet of card
- Cartridge paper
- Paints and paintbrushes

Cloth Poncho

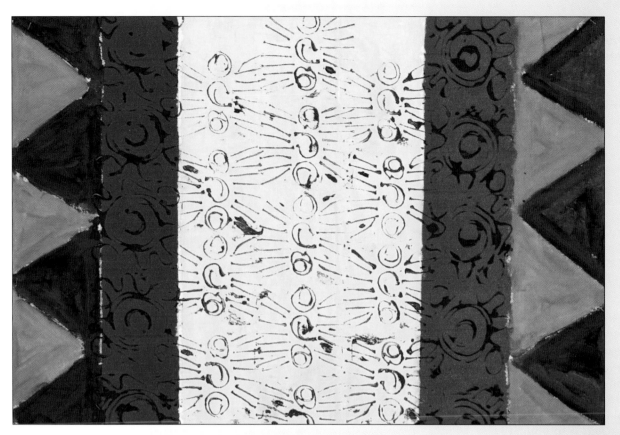

Most Mexicans in the towns and cities wear western-style clothes. Traditional dress is more often seen in villages and during festivals. These folk costumes are colourful and sometimes embroidered, woven or sequinned. Each religion has its own distinctive set of designs and colours.

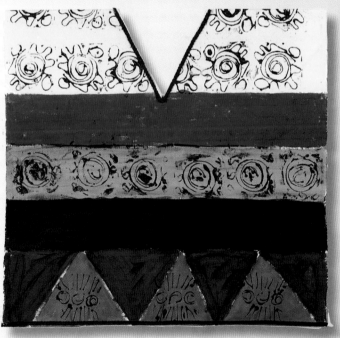

Resources
- Plastic table cloths
- Large piece of cotton fabric
- Fabric dyes
- Black paint and paintbrushes
- String
- Glue
- Card
- Fabric tape

Approach

1. Cover tables with plastic cloths and tape down the large sheet of fabric.

2. Mexican ponchos are often striped, with geometric designs. Look at examples and, in pencil, draw large striped patterns onto the cloth.

3. Paint the stripes in brightly coloured fabric dyes and allow to dry.

4. On a small piece of cardboard draw a small pattern in pencil. Cover the design with string and allow to dry. Carefully paint the string black and print onto the fabric.

5. To make the poncho, fold the fabric in half and cut out a triangle for the neck opening. Glue tape around the inside edges to prevent fraying.

Mexican Hat Dance

Dance forms an important part of Mexican culture. One of the most popular folk dances is the Mexican hat dance or the *Jarabe Tapatio*, a dance about courtship. The woman wears a brightly coloured full skirt, while the man dresses as a rodeo rider or *charro*. The man throws his hat – a wide-brimmed sombrero – on the floor and dances around it. The woman puts the hat on her head to show she accepts him. They dance the finale together.

Resources
- Paper plates
- Plastic cups
- Cellulose paste powder and water
- Scrap paper
- Paints and paintbrushes
- Feathers, sequins and other decorative materials
- Painted cloth

Approach

1. Place an upturned plastic cup in the middle of a plate. Cover the whole plate and cup together with a layer or two of papier-mâché. This should be sufficient to attach the cup firmly to the base of the plate. Allow to dry.

2. Paint the hat in bold designs and bright colours.

3. Decorate the hat with feathers, sequins or other materials.

4. Display several hats as a huge sombrero with a large painted cloth circle as the centre.

Frida Kahlo Self-portraits

Frida Kahlo (1907–1954) was born in a small village just outside Mexico City. At the age of 18 Kahlo was involved in a bus accident that resulted in several broken bones and damage to her spine. She managed to walk again, but suffered from her injuries throughout her life. Confined to bed during her convalescence, boredom led her to start painting and she produced many self-portraits. She was celebrated during her lifetime and has become one of Mexico's most famous artists.

Approach

1. Retell the story of the life of Frida Kahlo and discuss the inspiration behind her art.

The Frame, 1938, by Frida Kahlo (1907–1954)
© Agence Photographique RMN

Resources

- Pictures of portraits by Frida Kahlo
- Pencils
- Mirrors
- Paints and paintbrushes
- Coloured paper
- Glue

2. Show pictures of her portraits and encourage the children to engage with them by asking questions. What mood do you think she is in? How old do you think she is? What is happening in the background?

3. Talk to the children about the general proportions of a face. Draw an oval and demonstrate how the eyes would fall approximately at mid-point and that halfway between the eyes and lower part of the oval would be the nose, and so on.

4. Emphasise that, although we all have the same basic features, our individual facial movements and expressions give us our own distinctive character. Give children a mirror to study carefully their own faces.

5. In her self-portrait, *The Frame*, Kahlo created a frame of brightly coloured birds and flowers. Ask the children to consider what sort of frame they are going to create.

6. Ask the children to sketch out their own self-portrait in pencil and paint, in the style of Kahlo.

7. Create a border of vibrant flowers and birds.

Mountain Questions

Show the children a large world map with all the major mountain ranges featured. Can they identify any of them? Give the children the names of the mountains and a selection of atlases. Ask them to try to match up the names of the mountains to the larger world map. Brainstorm what the children already know about some of these mountains or mountains in general. Encourage questions about mountains and find out if the children can predict answers to any of the questions.

Approach

1. Fold a large piece of cardboard vertically in half and cut out jagged peaks.

2. Using a variety of card and collage material, add to the mountains to give a 3-D effect.

3. Create further mountainous shapes by folding smaller pieces of card and standing them in front of the main structure.

4. Word process the questions in large type and stick them onto card. Cut the question cards into jagged shapes and stick them onto the mountain.

5. Another mountain could be created with the answers displayed in a similar way.

Resources
- Large map of the world
- Atlases
- Large sheet of cardboard
- Collage materials
- Glue

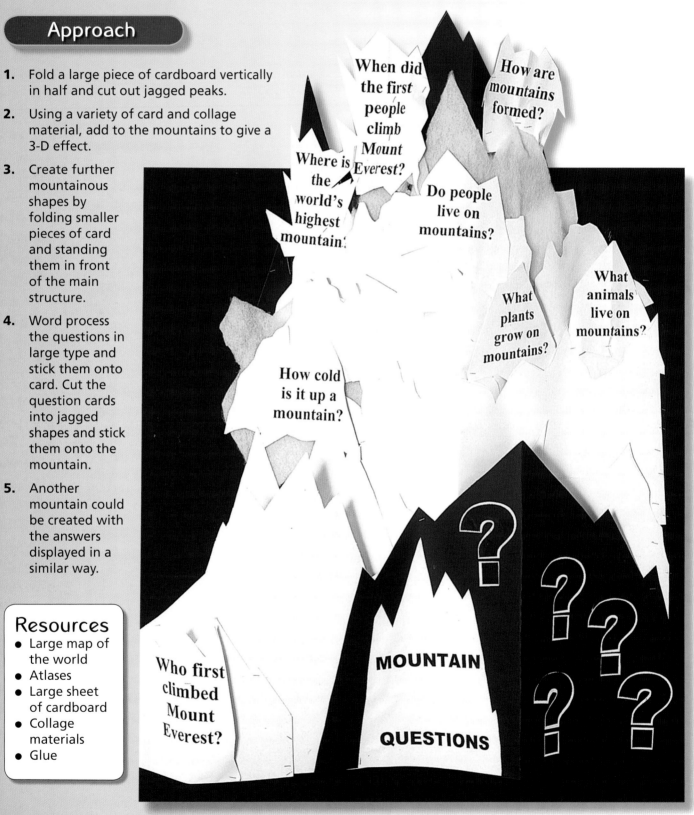

Contour Maps

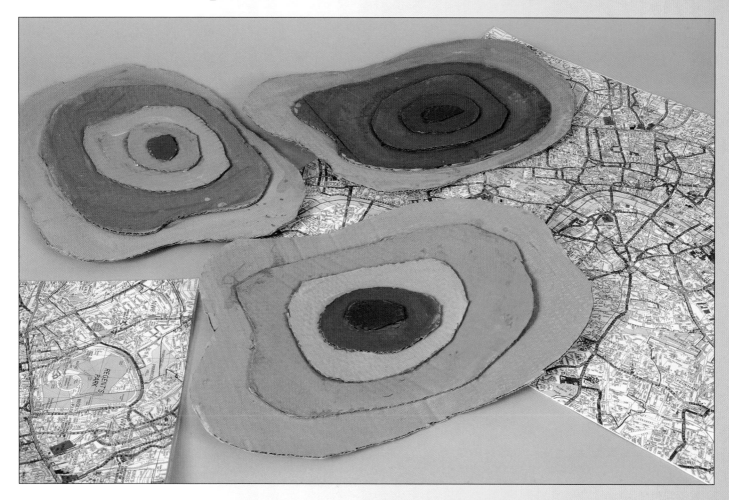

Contours are a two-dimensional way of showing the height of land on a map. Contour lines join up places that are all the same height and show how many metres above sea level they are.

Approach

1. Begin by showing how mapmakers draw lines on maps. Explain how all coastlines are at sea level, at 0 metres. Allow the children time to examine maps of hilly and flat areas and explore the differences in the contour lines.

2. Give each child a photocopy of a simple contour map.

3. Demonstrate how to turn this into a relief map by cutting out the largest area first and using it as a stencil to cut out a piece of card. Cut out the next contour and again use it as a stencil to cut a piece of card the same size. Repeat until all the contours have been cut out in card.

4. Stick all the pieces of card into the correct position and paint so that the highest point is the darkest.

5. As an extension, children could design their own contour map, putting on map symbols and recreating it as a 3-D model.

Resources
- Photocopies of a simple contour map
- Sheets of fairly thick card
- Paints and paintbrushes
- Glue

Mountain Landscapes

Pictorial representations of space and form fascinate David Hockney (born 1937) and landscapes are a recurring subject in his art. His series of paintings of hills and mountains show vibrant landscapes in vivid contrasting colours.

Resources
- Reproductions of Hockney's art
- Photographs of mountainous and hilly scenes
- Paint and paintbrushes
- Collage materials
- Glue

Approach

1. Look at the painting of David Hockney's hills and mountains. Discuss the shapes, patterns and choice of colours.

2. Working from photographs of similar views, ask children to sketch out a drawing in the style of David Hockney.

3. Paint in bright colours.

4. As a supplementary activity, children could create a textile/collage version of the scene. Try to find some unusual collage materials for added interest.

The Road Across the Wolds, 1997 by David Hockney (1937–), Oil on canvas 48x60" © David Hockney

Rocky Mountain Geology

The rocks that exist nowadays on the earth have been formed in many different ways. Many minerals found in rocks are mined because they are useful to us; some are very valuable. Diamonds, coal, gemstones and some metals, such as gold, are all examples of minerals found in rocks.

Resources

- Margarine tub
- Modelling material
- Rocks and minerals
- Paints and paintbrushes
- Plaster of Paris and water

Approach

1. Begin by putting a layer of modelling material 2–3cm thick at the bottom of a margarine tub.

2. Choose a mineral and press it firmly into the modelling material, making sure to leave a clear impression.

3. Mix up some plaster of Paris by gradually adding the powder to water until it has the consistency of thin custard.

4. Pour the mixture into the tub and leave for an hour or two until set.

5. Break away the plastic tub and peel off the modelling material.

6. Paint the model to match the colours of the chosen mineral.

Photographic Mountains

The special qualities of photography make it an ideal medium to create life-like pictures of mountains enveloped in mist.

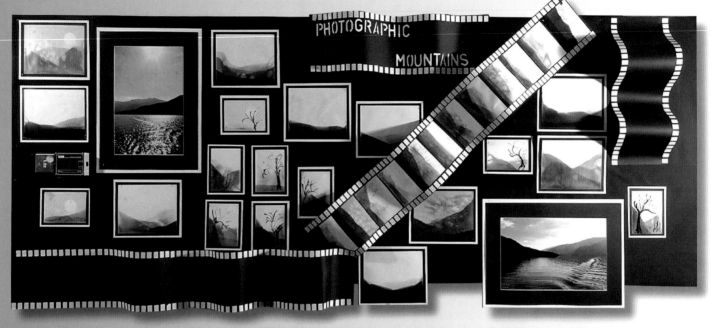

Resources
- Three plastic trays
- Developer
- Fixer
- Tongs
- Photographic paper
- Paintbrushes

Approach

1. Fill one plastic tray with water. Following the instructions on the bottles, mix the developer with water in another tray, and mix the fixer with water in the third tray.

2. Explain to the children about the qualities of photographic paper; once it is exposed to light it will start to react and colour. It is important to caution them about using chemicals. Although perfectly safe if handled correctly, they should not go near the eyes or mouth.

3. Remove a sheet of photographic paper from its black bag and paint on the outline of a tree, using a paintbrush dipped in developer.

4. Working fairly quickly, dip the same sheet of photographic paper into the developer diagonally, a few centimetres at a time, to make the mountain shapes. Avoid plunging the whole sheet into the developer.

5. Using tongs, submerge the sheet of photographic paper fully into the fixer tray for about five minutes.

6. Remove the photographic paper from the fixer and put it in the final tray of water for at least 10 minutes. Dry flat.

7. The resulting images will be highly atmospheric and may inspire some ideas that could be a source for poetry.

Snowboard Designs

Snowboards or 'snurfers', as they were originally called in the 1960s when they were first designed, are a cross between a skateboard, a surfboard and a ski.

Resources
- Long pieces of cardboard
- Paints
- Paintbrushes
- Black paper
- Glue

Approach

1. Look at a range of skiwear and discuss the patterns and colours that are used. The clothes are usually in vibrant colours, with bold patterns.

2. Ask the children how they might design a range of winter sportswear and equipment. Prepare a design sheet of possible ideas and colours.

3. Draw a design for a snowboard onto the cardboard. Paint it in bright colours.

4. Glue on foot straps made from black paper and display as shown.

Features and Creatures

WHICH COASTAL FEATURE IS HOME TO EACH OF THESE COASTAL CREATURES?

Resources
- Maps and atlases
- Cartridge paper
- Paints and paintbrushes
- Card
- Collage materials

The coast or seashore is where the sea meets the land. Give the children maps and atlases and locate coastlines around the world. Discuss how coasts differ depending on their location. Most seashores share a common element in that they are home to all kinds of wildlife, from tiny crabs and snails to turtles and large seabirds. Ask the children to research seashore creatures and find out as much as they can about their habitat and way of life.

Approach

1. Give each child a large sheet of cartridge paper. Challenge them to paint a background in as many different shades of blue as possible. Encourage them to try and get some movement into the sea by painting wavy lines.

2. When dry, staple the sheets of paper to the display board in a way that creates 3-D waves.

3. Cut out some large wave shapes, paint them and display above the board.

4. Ask the children to choose a sea creature to research. Ask them to draw and paint it onto card. Add collage material if required.

5. Cut out the creatures and display them on the sea background.

6. Encourage the children to explain to the class about the creatures on the display and talk about the features of the coastal environment in which they live.

Shell Designs

Show the children a collection of shells. Ask questions that will enhance the children's powers of observation and encourage artistic vocabulary, for example: What are the darkest and lightest tones on the shells? Is the texture rough, smooth, jagged, pointed? What shape are the shells?

Resources
- Shells
- Coloured paper
- Viewfinders
- Drawing media

Approach

1. Challenge the children to draw samples of sections of a shell, concentrating on patterns and textures. Offer viewfinders and a choice of size and colour of paper and of pencils, pens, charcoal or crayons. Encourage them to use the drawing media as experimentally as possible. Ask: What is the lightest, darkest, smoothest or most jagged mark that can be made?

2. Use a photocopier to enlarge parts of the children's designs, and to make repeat patterns. Encourage the process of stylising drawings or parts of drawings. Demonstrate how the simplest of marks can make an interesting design.

3. With the photocopied drawings encourage the children to reproduce a shell pattern using a variety of drawing media or screen printing techniques.

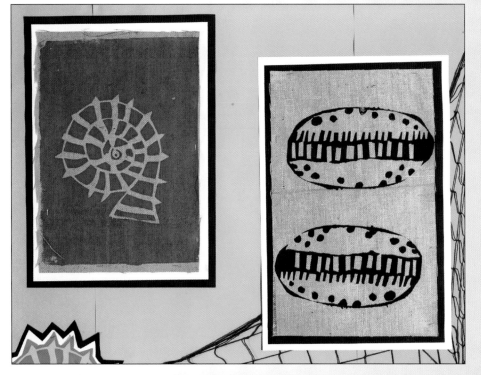

Coastal Frieze

Henri Matisse (1869–1954) created some of his most imaginative works using sheets of cut paper. Paper cut-outs make bold, strong images; the simple designs are hugely effective. His 1946 work *Polynesia, The Sea*, shown below, helps children appreciate the enormous diversity of plants and animals that live in or near water. Talk about the images that can be seen in the painting.

Approach

1. Ask the children to research animals and plants that live in the sea.

2. Look again at Matisse's style. Choose two or three creatures and demonstrate how to simplify their shapes.

3. Provide the children with white cartridge paper to draw their simplified birds, fish or seaweed. Cut out the shapes.

4. Cover a large sheet of cartridge paper with rectangles of blue paper, alternating the two shades.

5. Arrange the paper cut-outs on top of the blue background. When satisfied with the composition stick them down firmly.

6. A large wall-hanging version could be made in fabric using the same technique.

Resources
- Two shades of blue paper
- White cartridge paper
- Glue
- Silk screens, squeegee and fabric (optional)

Screen Print Creatures

As an extension, the bold simplified shapes of sea creatures can be developed into a screen-printed picture (shown centre of display, above).

1. Prepare a stencil by drawing sea creatures and seaweed onto plain paper.

2. Cut out the shapes and discard the rest of the paper.

3. Place the shapes onto the fabric, lower the screen over the top and use a squeegee to pull the paint evenly from the top of the screen to the bottom. This may take two or three pulls.

4. Remove the screen; the paper stencils will stick to the screen leaving the background printed.

5. Repeat this process with as many designs as required to make the picture.

Polynesia, The Sea, 1946, by Henri Matisse (1869–1954) © Photo CNAC/MNAM Dist. RMN

Environmental Sculptures

Artists like Andy Goldsworthy (born 1956 in Cheshire, England) are called 'environmental sculptors'. Their works are made from things found in nature that come immediately to hand, and nothing else. They create their art without causing any damage to the environment. A visit to the coast would be ideal to inspire the children to create an environmental sculpture using pebbles, driftwood, shells and rocks.

Resources
- Seaside objects
- Camera
- Pictures of environmental sculptures

Approach

1. Show the children pictures of environmental sculptures by Andy Goldsworthy. Discuss the way natural objects have been arranged and what he has chosen to create the sculpture.

2. Ask the children to arrange their shells, driftwood, seaweed or other objects in an original way, referring back to some of Andy Goldsworthy's examples.

3. The children's work could be photographed and then left on the beach, as the true essence of this genre of work is for it to merge back into the natural environment.

4. Explain to the children that environmental sculptures are not meant to be permanent. Ask them to sketch a picture of their finished sculpture and give it a title.

Anglo-Saxon Village

Two thousand years ago Britain was inhabited by people called Celts. Most of the Celts were farmers and lived in small villages, in groups called tribes. Over the next thousand years, Britain was invaded by the Romans, Anglo-Saxons and Vikings, all of whom stayed and provided many of the settlements that we use today.

Approach

1. Dip the plaster bandages into a tray of water for 3–4 seconds, then stick them onto a large sheet of cardboard to create an uneven effect to represent a field.

2. Allow the field to dry, then paint it green.

3. Mould strips of modelling material and press painted lolly sticks into it to create a perimeter fence.

4. Show the children pictures of Anglo-Saxon houses and ask them to sketch some of the features.

5. Demonstrate how to make cuboids out of thin card and suggest ways of making the roof. Cover the roof in lolly sticks and art straws. Paint.

6. Put the village together, referring to diagrams based on research.

7. Give the children a list of Anglo-Saxon words, for example:

   ton farm/village, **ham** village/hamlet, **ing** folk/people of, **stead** farm, **ford** river crossing, **wic** farm, **burk** fort, **worth** enclosure.

   Ask the children to create a name for their village.

Resources
- Thin card
- Cardboard
- Modroc plaster bandages
- Water tray
- Modelling material
- Lolly sticks
- Art straws
- Glue
- Paints and paintbrushes

Mapping the Village

Aerial views can provide a starting point for basic map work with young children. There are two types of aerial photographs: vertical and oblique. A vertical photograph (or plan) is taken from directly above, while an oblique photograph is taken from the side. A vertical photograph of the model Anglo-Saxon village will provide the outline for mapping the position of its features.

Approach

1. Show the children the aerial view photographs of the model Anglo-Saxon village. Point out how the shapes of the buildings change when looked upon from above. Compare the vertical and oblique views. Discuss what looks strange or cannot be identified.

2. Trace the shapes and features of the village and, if necessary, enlarge the photograph on a photocopier.

3. Colour the shapes and make a key to show what the different coloured shapes are.

4. As an extension activity, add grid squares to help the children say where the features are on the Anglo-Saxon map. Encourage them to make up questions for each other to answer.

5. Compare the Anglo-Saxon mapped village with aerial photographs and maps of villages today. Discuss how they have changed.

Resources
- Vertical and oblique photographs of the model village
- Tracing paper
- Crayons

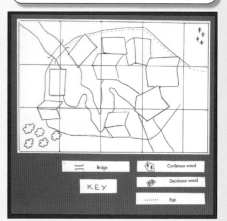

Viking Wattle Wall-hanging

Archaeologists have found that some of the walls of Viking houses were made of wattle. Wattle is made by weaving twigs or sticks in and out of pieces of wood stuck in the ground.

Resources
- Fabric scraps
- Sticks and twigs
- Thin wire and cutters
- Glue

Approach

1. Make a collection of sticks and twigs and scraps of felt, woollen and hessian fabric.

2. Demonstrate how to attach the sticks to the fabric, using thin wire, and how to weave the thinner twigs between them. Soaking the twigs in water will make them more pliable and less likely to snap.

3. Show examples of how people have used natural objects to make visual structures and wall-hangings. Encourage the children to sketch out ideas around a chosen theme, for example, autumn leaves, bluebell woods or poppy fields.

4. Children could work individually or in a group to produce a structure that represents their chosen theme. Encourage the children to consider how their choice of materials represents parts of their visual theme.

Roman Road

When the Romans settled in Britain they built the first real roads. They built them as straight as possible to carry goods and for the rapid movement of troops. They had frequent milestones and posthouses.

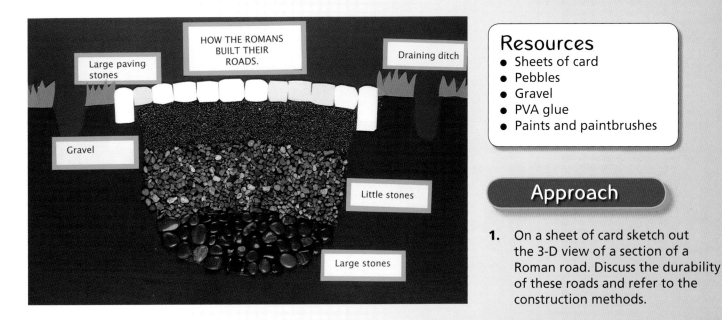

Resources
- Sheets of card
- Pebbles
- Gravel
- PVA glue
- Paints and paintbrushes

Approach

1. On a sheet of card sketch out the 3-D view of a section of a Roman road. Discuss the durability of these roads and refer to the construction methods.

2. Using strong PVA glue, attach the pebbles in the different layers, with the largest at the bottom, and finishing with gravel at the top.

3. Paint the road and label the layers.

Modern Road Signs

Resources
- Card
- Copies of road signs
- Paints and paintbrushes

1. Compare the road network of today's villages, towns and cities with the Roman period. Look at modern construction methods and road signs. Discuss the need for so many signs today, compared with the milestones of Roman Britain.

2. Ask the children to study the road signs and choose a simple one to print onto a piece of card. Cut out the signs and display.

3. Challenge the children to design their own road signs for a busy Roman road, considering the type and volume of traffic using it.

World Climate

Talk about where the children go on holiday. Locate these places on a large map of the world. Discuss the climate in each area and whether this is a deciding factor in where people go. Explain that the world can be divided into climate zones and that the weather will be different in each of these zones at any given time. Divide the class into groups and give each group a different climate zone to research, for example, polar region or rainforest. Make a list of questions for the children to find about the weather in each zone, such as: What is the average temperature, rainfall and number of hours of sunshine?

Resources

- World map
- Display board
- Card
- Black paper
- Collage materials
- Paints and paintbrushes
- String

Approach

1. Prepare the display board by covering it in black paper.

2. Cut out a large paper circle and draw an outline map of the world on it. The children could paint the map or cover it in tissue paper to show the land and sea areas. Cut out smaller circles from card, one for each climate zone group.

3. Ask the children to design a collage to depict some of the characteristics of the region they have researched. Ideas could include temperature, vegetation or cultural heritage.

4. Give the children a selection of collage materials and paints to create their picture.

5. Label the area or country of research and link it to the world map with string.

6. Ask the children to give the rest of the class a more detailed report of their climate zone, saying whether or not they would like to visit the place.

Isobars

An isobar is a line on a weather map that joins together all the places with the same air pressure. The closer the isobars, the stronger the winds. If the isobars are spread widely it means light winds. Winds blow exactly parallel to the isobars.

Resources
- Black paper
- Grey paint and paintbrushes
- White string and glue
- Pictures of isobar weather maps

Approach

1. Ask the children to trace or draw free hand a map of the UK on black paper and paint it grey.

2. Provide a range of weather maps with isobars on them. Ask the children to recreate a weather picture in isobars on their painted map, using string to represent the isobars.

3. Ask the children to write a weather forecast for their isobar picture. Display the maps as shown, using string to create the letters of the title.

Satellite Pictures

Weather satellites orbit the earth collecting information about global weather conditions. As well as helping us forecast weather, satellites can also be used to study the environment and monitor global warming.

Resources
- Cartridge paper
- Marbling ink and comb
- Water tray
- Satellite pictures of Earth
- Green paint and paintbrushes

Approach

1. Show the children examples of satellite pictures for the UK and the world. Explain how the cloud formations can help forecast the weather. Ask the children to predict what the weather is like for the countries in the examples.

2. Give each child a cartridge paper circle. Ask them to trace or draw a map of the world and to paint land areas green. Allow to dry.

3. Demonstrate the process of creating swirling storm conditions by dropping marbling ink into the water and 'combing' in circular movements.

4. Place the painted map face down on top of the swirling ink. Lift out and leave to dry.

5. Ask the children what the weather might be like for the countries under their satellite picture. Would it be a realistic weather condition for the various countries on their map?

Jack Frost Collage

Water, in its different forms, can be a stimulus for many art projects. Pictures and photographs of frost patterns may be used as a starting point for a sculptural frost collage.

Approach

1. Look at pictures of frost, and observe the shapes and patterns it forms.

2. Allow the children time to sketch out an imaginary face of Jack Frost, thinking about colours, shapes and facial expressions.

3. Either individually or in pairs, use papier-mâché to stick the plastic mask onto the background sheet of card.

4. Add features to the mask, for example, icicles dangling from the chin, in papier-mâché.

5. Use collage materials to add interest, referring back to sketch book ideas.

6. Paint or spray the collage appropriately. Use glitter and sequins to make Jack Frost sparkle.

Resources
- Card
- Collage materials
- Silver spray paint
- Sequins and glitter
- Cellulose paste powder and water
- Scrap paper
- Plastic masks

Frosty Fern Patterns

Fern frost forms on windows when dew freezes on cold glass and turns to ice. It creates feathery patterns when more moisture freezes on top in layers.

Approach

1. To screen paint the fern fronds, position a leaf on top of the paper or fabric.

2. Lower the screen on top of the leaf and ask a child to hold it down firmly.

3. Put the paint at one end of the screen. Ask another child to pull the paint evenly down to the other end of the screen with the squeegee. This may need two or three pulls.

4. Remove the screen and let the paint dry.

5. To make a simple fern print, paint one side of the leaf generously with paint.

Resources
- White, grey, blue and black paper
- Poster paint in cold colours
- Fern leaves, dried and pressed
- Silk screens and squeegee
- Glitter, sequins and silver thread
- Fabric (optional)
- Glue

6. Turn the leaf over and print onto the paper. Press firmly, then remove the leaf. Allow to dry.

7. Decorate with glitter, sequins or silver thread.

47

Ice Cubes

Water freezes to ice when its temperature drops below 0°C. Icebergs are giant slabs of ice that break away from the polar ice caps in warm weather. They float because ice is lighter than water, although only about 10% of an iceberg is visible above the water.

Resources
- Ice cubes
- Magnifying glass
- Carboard boxes (or card and net)
- Card or silver paper
- Collage materials and glue
- Paints and paintbrushes

Approach

1. Look at some cubes of ice. Examine the patterns using a magnifying glass. Study pictures of icebergs.

2. Create an ice cube collage. Give each child a box to decorate or a net to make their own cube.

3. Paint or spray the cube silver or white.

4. Build up patterns, exploring the textures of collage materials and shadows of paper sculpture to create ice shapes. Display the ice cubes against a background of 2-D ice patterns.

Fog Pictures

Condensation in the air near the ground forms moisture or fog. Fog tends to develop on clear cool nights, when moisture escapes from warm ground that is quickly cooling down.

Resources
- Cartridge paper
- Black crayons or paint
- Tracing paper
- Pictures of foggy weather

Approach

1. Show children pictures of foggy weather and talk about ways of making a picture appear foggy by overlapping layers of tracing paper. Demonstrate this process.

2. Ask children to produce a landscape picture on cartridge paper using only black pencil, crayon or grey/black paint.

3. Place a sheet of tracing paper over the landscape picture. It will immediately look distant and 'foggy'. Repeat the process for a greater 3-D effect.

Ray of Hope

Ozone is a protective gas cloud up in the atmosphere. It keeps out harmful rays from the sun and prevents the Earth getting too hot. This natural shield has been damaged over the past few decades by manufactured chemicals called CFCs. When this protective 'blanket' around us becomes too thin, or holes appear, it lets more ultraviolet (UV) rays through. Most experts believe the world's climate could start to change.

Resources

- Red, yellow or orange paper or card
- Collage materials and glue
- Cardboard egg trays
- Paints and paintbrushes
- Information about global warming

Approach

1. Cover a large circle in cardboard egg trays. Ask the children to paint it in bright, sunny colours.

2. Make large flames out of card. Paint them and allow to dry, then embellish with collage materials such as tissue paper, sequins and coloured pasta.

3. Glue the flames around the sun.

4. Add labels to the flames with the children's thoughts about global warming.

The Water Cycle

Talk about how the water we use today is the same water that was drunk by the dinosaurs 250 million years ago. Use diagrams to explain the recycling of our water. Show the path of evaporated seawater forming clouds, which travel across the land, eventually falling as rain into the rivers and back into the sea. Challenge the children to find the most unusual, controversial or alarming fact about water. The resulting work will prompt some interesting points and future research possibilities. Some of the facts could be written on raindrop-shaped paper and displayed around the water cycle diagram.

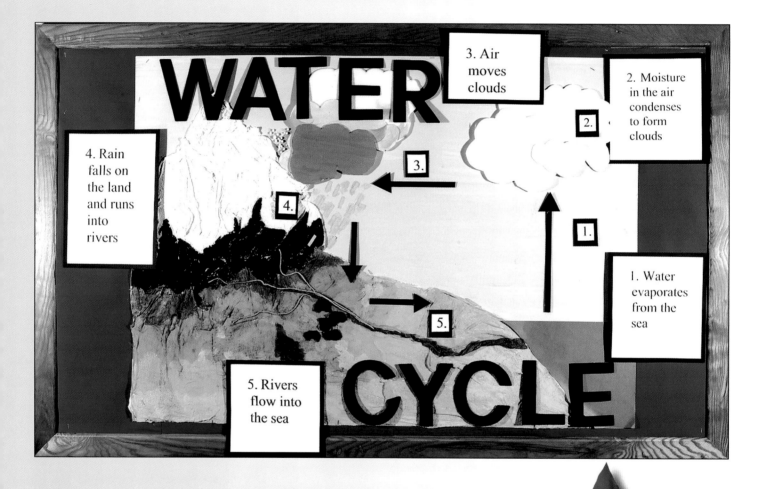

Approach

1. On a large piece of card draw the outline of a landscape showing mountains, hills, a river and the sea.

2. Use modroc to form the features of the mountains and hills, crinkling the wet plaster bandages to resemble mountain peaks. Allow the modroc to dry and it will stick firmly to the cardboard background.

3. Paint the landscape features, adding clouds, rain and snow. Add numbered arrows in appropriate positions to show the water cycle.

Resources
- Card
- Modroc plaster bandages
- Paints and paintbrushes

4. Type out the water cycle process and place these labels around the diagram.

5. Display some raindrops around the board, adding the water facts as they are researched throughout the topic. Children could suggest ways of categorising their facts and display accordingly.

Water Reflections

David Hockney (born 1937) moved from London to Los Angeles and painted images and scenes, which were particularly American for him. His series of paintings of swimming pools provides inspiration for this art activity.

Resources

- Photographs of reflections in swimming pools
- Paints and paintbrushes
- Cartridge paper and glue
- Viewfinders

Approach

1. Take photographs of reflections in swimming pools. Display them for the children to study and explain how we often look to nature for inspiration for design.

2. Study the photographs, comparing the patterns and shapes with Hockney's works.

3. Stick the photographs in the middle of a sheet of cartridge paper. Sketch out faintly the patterns made by water ripples, such as distorted swimming lane lines.

4. Ask the children to mix colours to match those in the photograph and extend the colour to the edge of the paper.

5. Ask the children to focus on one particular area of their photograph using a viewfinder.

6. Demonstrate how to simplify the patterns, focussing purely on the patterns and shapes of the reflections.

7. Enlarge ripple shapes onto a large sheet of cartridge paper and paint in shades of blue.

Le Plongeur (Paper Pool 18), 1978 by David Hockney (1937–), pressed paper pulp 71x171" © David Hockney

Tie and Dye Ripples

Resources
- Squares of cotton fabric
- Dried peas
- Elastic bands
- Blue dye and bucket
- Iron

Blow-painted Bubbles

Resources
- Plastic drinking straws
- Liquid detergent
- Powder paint
- Cartridge paper
- Circular plastic pots
- Blue paper

Approach

1. Demonstrate ways of folding or tying the fabric to create different patterns. For example, folding the cloth forwards and backwards in a concertina fashion will create a striped effect. Tying dried peas into the fabric randomly all over will give a ripple effect.

2. Ask the children to choose which style of tie and dye they are going to try. Stress the need to get the elastic bands as tight as possible.

3. When the fabric pieces are all tied, place them in a bucket of blue dye for at least an hour. When dry, iron flat (only an adult should use the iron).

4. Display the squares as a patchwork of ripples alongside the bubble paintings.

Approach

1. Prepare a mixture of powder paint, water and liquid detergent. Mix several shades of blue and pour the mixtures into different-sized plastic pots.

2. Provide each child with a plastic straw and demonstrate how to blow the mixture until the bubbles start to appear just above the rim of the container.

3. Print off the bubbles by placing the paper over them and pushing gently down. Repeat several times, building up a pattern of bubble prints.

4. Cut out the bubbles and display on a circular piece of paper, adding circles of blue paper to complete the pictures.

Bubble Relief Pictures

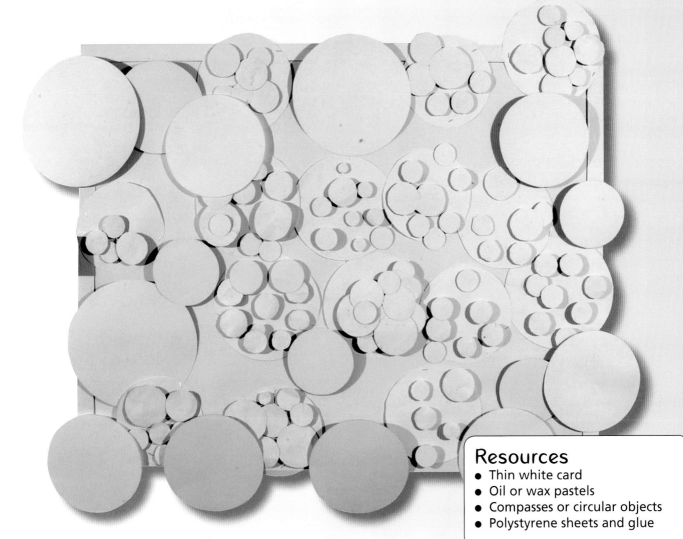

Resources
- Thin white card
- Oil or wax pastels
- Compasses or circular objects
- Polystyrene sheets and glue

Approach

1. Ask the children to draw and cut out several different-sized circles from thin card.

2. Colour one face of each circle in bright pastels.

3. Stick small squares of polystyrene together. Glue the polystyrene squares onto the coloured faces of the circles to raise them to different heights.

4. Glue the polystyrene squares onto the white backing card so that the coloured circles reflect subtly onto the white backing sheet.

Abstract Water Art

Resources
- Large sheet of card
- Pictures of water in different forms
- Paints and paintbrushes
- Collage materials
- Glue

Abstract art is non-representational. It attempts to convey meaning through abstract shapes or imagined forms, dramatically simplified. Explain to the children what abstract art is. Show examples of work by the Russian artist, Wassily Kandinsky (1866–1944) who wanted his art to make us think about our feelings, evoke moods and suggest meaning as music does. Stress that art is like a language and artists use their work to communicate ideas and messages.

Approach

1. Distribute around the class a variety of water pictures in contrasting styles. Ask the children to describe how the artists have interpreted the theme of water. Discuss the ways in which the artists have created the mood of the water and if they have tried to reproduce exactly what they see.

2. Discuss how abstract art portrays feeling – moods can be important subjects for paintings and can produce powerful images.

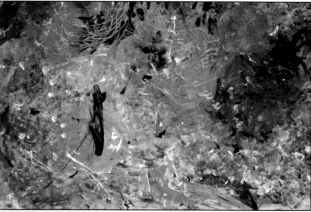

3. Brainstorm images of water, from fast-flowing waterfalls to calm lily ponds, bubbles, reflections, ice and choppy seas. Ask the children to suggest shapes to represent the different forms of water.

4. Experiment, making marks and squiggles, to discover which ones convey movement or create feelings. Stress how different shapes, lines and patterns can conjure up various emotions in the viewer.

5. Use the children's ideas to create an imaginative collage based on the theme of water. Suggest to the children that they may wish to choose one particular form of water to portray.

Tissue Paper Fish

Resources
- Laminated pouches
- Tissue paper in various shades
- Glue
- Circle templates

Approach

1. Laminate sheets of tissue paper.

2. Give the children different-sized circles to draw around and cut out of the laminated sheets.

3. Draw the outline of a large fish on a sheet of paper.

4. Starting at the tail end of the fish, overlap the circles and glue them together, taking care not to stick them to the paper outline.

5. When dry add features such as eyes. Lift the fish off the paper outline and display it against a window to get the full effect of the overlapping shades of tissue paper.

Island Life

Read *Katie Morag's Island Stories* by Mairi Hedderwick (published by Red Fox) about an island home. The Isle of Struay is an imaginary island in Scotland. Locate Scotland on a map of the UK and relate it to the children's home. Discuss who lives in Struay and what work they do. How does it differ from work in a city? Look at the map of Struay and find out about the places named; for example, what is a jetty? Look at the features of the island environment and discuss how they are similar to, or different from, their own locality. Looking at a map of the UK, suggest ways of reaching Struay from the mainland and what the journey may be like. Ask the children whether they would prefer to visit Struay in the winter or summer, and why.

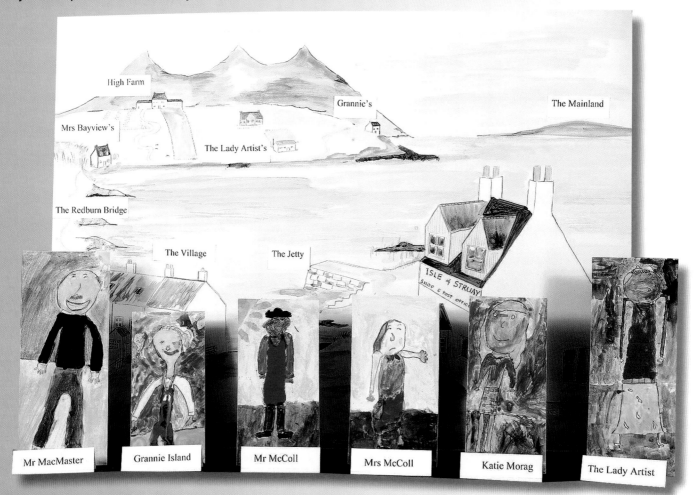

Approach

1. On a large piece of card draw the outline of a scene in Struay that can be found on the inside cover of most Katie Morag stories about the island. Discuss what time of year the painting is to portray and paint accordingly.

2. List the main characteristics of the island and make suggestions as to who else may live there; let the children invent new characters.

3. Ask the children to choose one of their own characters or an established main character to draw and paint. Cut out the figures and add them to the landscape of Struay.

4. As each new character is added to the picture, find out where they live and what they do for a living.

5. Add animals to the island and talk about their part in island life.

Resources
- *Katie Morag's Island Stories* (Red Fox)
- Card
- Paints and paintbrushes

Souvenir Painting

Many people living in islands like Struay rely heavily on tourism as a form of income, and landscape art is a popular souvenir from picturesque places. Ask the children to imagine what life on Struay is like. Look at the main display and ask them to think that they are standing outside the shop, looking out to sea. What would they see? Encourage geographical observation with questions. Is the area built up, mountainous or flat? Is the sea rough or calm? Look at the pictures of the Isle of Struay in Mairi Hedderwick's *Katie Morag's Island Stories*. Pick out clues about the landscape and discuss what media were used to illustrate them.

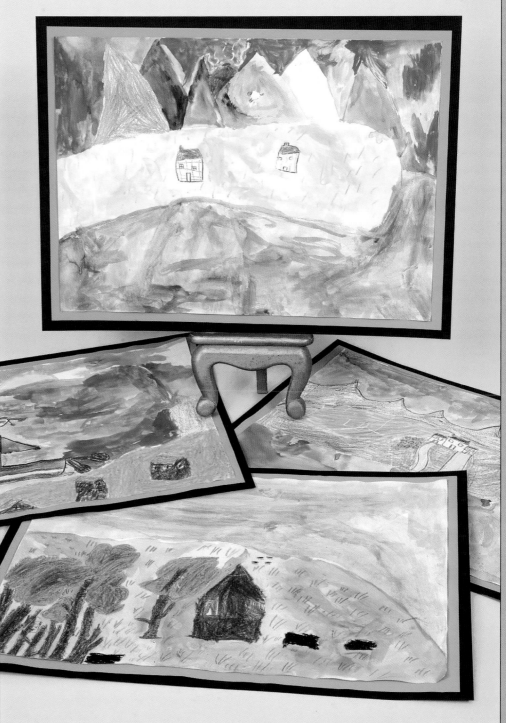

Resources
- Wax crayons
- Watercolours
- Cartridge paper
- Paintbrushes
- *Katie Morag's Island Stories* (Red Fox)

Approach

1. Explain to the children that mixed media art is when an artist uses several types of material in a piece of work.

2. Demonstrate the properties of watercolours and wax crayons and allow the children time to experiment using the two materials together.

3. Ask the children to imagine they are artists living on the island and they want to produce a piece of work to sell in the gift shop for tourists to buy. Talk about the sort of landscape they might portray.

4. Show the children how to produce a colour wash with the watercolours for the background to the landscape. Demonstrate the effect produced by drawing with the wax crayons and colour washing over the top.

Boat Designs

Look again at *Katie Morag's Island Stories* and discuss with the children all the different types of boats featured, from the large ferry to fishing boats and rowing boats. Talk about the sizes, the designs and the function of each type of boat.

Approach

1. Bring in some model boats. Encourage the children to study them from different perspectives and talk about how they might have been made.

2. Provide a collection of assorted cardboard boxes and modelling material. Consider how the scrap materials could be used as part of their model. Demonstrate ways of joining materials together with flaps, glue or tape.

3. Ask the children to sketch out a simple boat design and talk about what features it will have.

4. With the children working in pairs or individually, ask them to construct their boat and, when dry, to paint and decorate it.

5. Compare the different boat designs.

Resources
- Model boats
- Assorted cardboard boxes
- Scrap materials
- Modelling material
- Glue and tape
- Paints and paintbrushes
- *Katie Morag's Island Stories* (Red Fox)

Honeycomb

As islands are cut off from the mainland, islanders mainly rely on farming and fishing to make a living. Animals and wildlife would play an important role in the lives of the people of Struay. The island shop would sell the eggs from the chickens, the milk from the cows and home-made produce such as cheese, jam and honey from the bees that feast on the flowers around Struay.

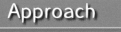 Approach

Resources
- Cartridge paper
- Black tissue paper
- Glue
- Paints
- Paintbrushes

1. Draw and cut out a large hexagon shape from cartridge paper for each child. Explain that the cells made by worker bees have six sides and tessellate neatly together.

2. Ask children to sketch patterns onto their hexagons in pencil.

3. By providing only yellow and red paint, challenge the children to mix as many different shades of orange as possible and to paint the pattern using just these colours.

4. Cut out circles in cartridge paper and ask the children to draw and paint alternate black and yellow stripes. Attach the bees' wings made from black tissue paper.

5. Put the hexagons together and display as a large honeycomb with the bees swarming over it.

Postcards

Explain to the children that seashores around the world vary enormously. Make a collection of postcards from resorts, showing different features and climates. Alternatively, photographs from travel brochures could be made into postcards. Find the seashores on a world map and discuss the features of each location. Tell the children that the seashore is a place where the sea or ocean meets the land but that not all the seashores of the world would make good holiday locations. Discuss the reasons for this. Using the children's own memories and recollections of seaside holidays, and referring to brochures and postcards from around the world, create a large group postcard showing different visual interpretations of life by the sea.

Resources
- Seaside postcards
- World map
- Card
- Black paper
- Paints and crayons
- Glue

Approach

1. Give each child a small piece of card on which to design a postcard.

2. Discuss the various images they could choose to draw on their card and show examples.

3. Ask the children to make a simple drawing of their seaside resort. Allow a choice of media to colour them.

4. Collect all the pictures together and stick them down on a large sheet of card.

5. Cover the display board in white paper and edge in black to resemble a stamp. Complete with a large silhouette of the queen's head in black paper.

Sandcastles

Looking at coastal fortifications and castles around the coastlines of the UK will inspire the designs of these sandcastle models.

Resources
- Polystyrene cups in different sizes
- Paint and paintbrushes
- PVA glue
- Card
- Sand

Approach

1. Ask the children to make a pencil sketch of a castle.

2. Demonstrate how the polystyrene cups can be combined or cut down to make interesting castle shapes.

3. Mix a little PVA glue into the paint, then paint the castles before gluing them onto the cardboard base.

4. Sprinkle a little sand on the model while the paint is still wet.

Windbreaks

There are plenty of brightly coloured beach accessories available to make a day at the seaside safer and more comfortable.

Resources
- Cartridge paper or fabric
- Wooden sticks
- Paints and paintbrushes

Approach

1. Fold a rectangular piece of paper into three or four sections and ask the children to draw a simple design using only a pencil and ruler.

2. Allow a choice of just three colours to paint the windbreak. Give the children time to experiment and choose which three colours go well together.

3. Paint the windbreak and allow to dry. Glue the sticks into the folds and at each end of the windbreak and display.

Lighthouses

Lighthouses built at sea are called rock lighthouses. They are situated on rocky reefs or small islands. Lighthouses mark hidden treacherous rocks, sandbanks and other dangers around the coast.

Approach

Resources
- Plastic bottles
- Paper
- Cardboard
- Modroc plaster bandages
- Paints and paintbrushes
- Glue

1. Attach an empty plastic bottle to the cardboard base using strips of modroc dipped in water, wrung out, and wound around the bottom of the bottle.

2. Use modroc to create rocks and waves around the bottom of the lighthouse. Paint.

3. Cover the main body of the bottle in paper and paint in red and white stripes.

4. Challenge the children to suggest materials to make up the rest of the structure of the lighthouse, referring to pictures. They could make it light up, using a bulb and simple circuit.

Sunglasses

Look at a collection of designs for spectacle frames and sunglasses, including the more outrageous versions worn on stage by Elton John and Dame Edna Everage.

Resources
- Card
- Cellophane
- Felt pens or crayons
- Glue

Approach

1. Ask the children to make a pencil design of a fantastic pair of sunglasses.

2. Provide each child with a sheet of A4 card with two holes cut out for the eyes. Ask them to draw on their design, cut out and colour.

3. Collage materials and extra card could be stuck on to make the glasses more extravagant.

4. On the reverse side of the glasses stick a sheet of cellophane to cover the eyeholes.

Sunhat

Approach

Resources
- Cellulose paste powder and water
- Scrap paper
- Balloons
- Card and glue
- Paints and paintbrushes

1. Blow up a balloon and cover the top half with papier-mâché.

2. When dry, pop the balloon and trim around the papier-mâché.

3. To make a brim, cut out a large circle in card. Place the papier-mâché crown in the centre of the large circle and draw around it.

4. Cut out the centre circle, leaving a couple of centimetres of card to snip and fold back inside the papier-mâché crown to attach it to the brim.

5. Decorate the sunhat and display with the sunglasses.

Bird's Eye View

Explain to the children that there are two main types of aerial photograph: a vertical view, which is like a plan, taken directly above the land; and an oblique view that shows the front and side of the area. Show examples of both types of photograph. If possible, show the children an aerial view of the school. Discuss whether it is a vertical or an oblique view. Talk about how shapes change when looked at from different perspectives. Look out for any mysterious features that the children do not recognise.

Resources

- Aerial photographs
- White and blue paper
- Glue
- Crayons or felt pens

Approach

1. Cut out a paper bird shape for each child.

2. Ask the children to imagine they are birds, flying over their school. What would they see? Refer to the aerial photographs and ask them to sketch and colour in the view from above onto their cut-out bird. Very young children will probably find it easier to show the school as an oblique view, portraying some of the features of the school and giving a more realistic perspective of the building.

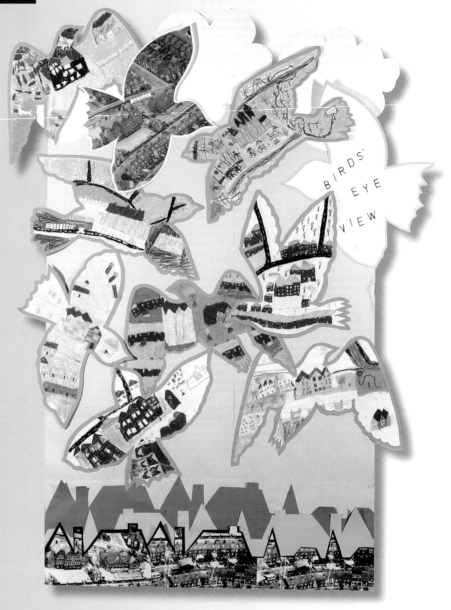

3. Cover the display board with blue paper. In the foreground, glue cut-out shapes of local buildings from photocopied aerial photographs.

4. Add the birds to the display, along with clouds and other sky features that the children feel are appropriate.

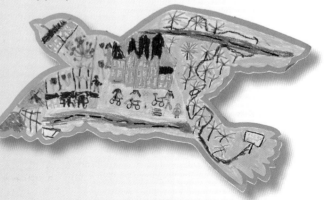

Map Symbols

Resources
- Polystyrene printing sheets
- Copies of map symbols
- Paints and paintbrushes
- Paper

Approach

1. Study a collection of map symbols and discuss what they represent.

2. Ask the children to each choose a symbol and practise drawing it.

3. Demonstrate how to indent the symbol onto a piece of polystyrene printing sheet. Ask the children to copy your method with the symbol they have chosen.

4. Cover the designs with paint and print onto a piece of paper.

Street Collage

Secondary sources of evidence, for example, photographs, are an excellent tool for enhancing the teaching and learning of Geography. Looking at photographs of the children's immediate locality will help to stimulate discussions and act as a starting point for interpreting what geographical clues and information a photograph can provide.

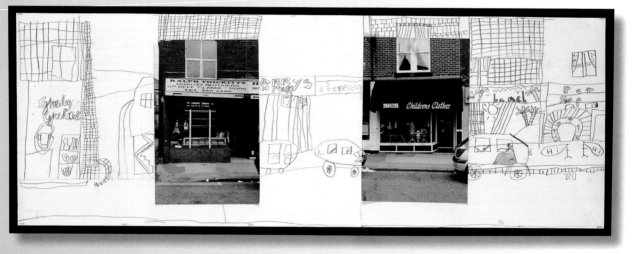

Approach

1. Encourage the children to study the photographs of a street near their school. Ask them to say what information they provide about the area as a whole.

2. Explain that the photograph is a small section of the local area. If they were to send it to children in another country they would not be able to see, for example, what was next to, or behind, the shops. What photographs do not show can be just as important as what they do show in terms of information about an area.

3. Show pictures of a more distant environment and ask the children to imagine what is immediately just outside the photograph.

Resources
- Camera
- Photographs of local streets
- Cartridge paper

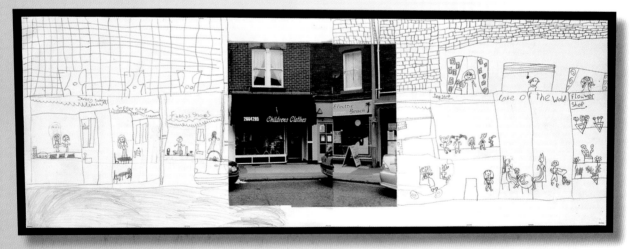

4. Make studies of shop fronts near your school. Directly observed sketches would be ideal but if not practical, take photographs.

5. Challenge the children to develop the street scene, working from observational recordings, from memory or by exercising their imagination.

6. If working from a photograph, provide a small part of the street scene and ask the children to put it in context by drawing what is next to, above and below it.

7. Talk about the difference between working from observation and working from memory or imagination.

Aerial Patterns

Asking children to look down at the ground provides a good starting point to discuss the perspective of aerial views and photographs.

Resources
- Thin white paper
- Wax crayons
- Camera

Approach

1. Take a walk around the school grounds, stopping every now and then to look down at patterns formed by brickwork, gratings, manhole covers and other features.

2. Look out for lines, motifs, repetition of shapes, and patterns. Make some rubbings using thick wax crayons on thin white paper.

3. Back in the classroom, develop the rubbings into patterns and drawings.

4. If possible, use aerial photographs to continue the patterns from this perspective.

River Journey

Begin by explaining the journey of a river from its source to the sea. A river is a large stream of fresh water, which starts at the source and flows downhill towards the sea or another river. Most rivers start high in the mountains and a stream flows quickly downhill. As it grows bigger it is joined by other streams and small rivers called tributaries. At this stage they often flow quickly in steep, narrow valleys; plunging waterfalls and white water rapids are common. A river becomes deeper and wider as it gets closer to the sea and meanders across wide, flat valleys. Sometimes, when the river floods, water flows across the land between two loops of a meander and straightens its courses. This cuts off the meander and creates an oxbow lake. The flat land near a river that floods, is called the flood plain. The soil is very fertile around this area. Eventually the river meets the sea, where it is called the mouth of the river.

Resources
- Card
- Blue tissue paper
- Glue
- Paints and paintbrushes

Approach

1. Type out the major river words in the journey and mount them onto card.

2. Draw a large picture of a mountain scene, with the tree line showing a mixture of coniferous and deciduous woods.

3. Recreate the river journey, using scrunched-up tissue paper. Try to create as many different river features as possible on the picture.

4. Display the words around the river. Encourage the children to match up the words to the features. Children could draw their own river map and add more words and features as the topic progresses.

Waterfalls

When the land that a river is travelling over suddenly changes level, the water flows over the ledge into the pool below, creating a waterfall. The Japanese artist Katushika Hokusai (1760–1849) produced a set of prints of waterfalls that show a fascination for the various ways in which water behaves (see the example below).

Resources
- Pictures of Hokusai's waterfall prints
- Card
- Tissue paper
- String
- Glue
- Paints and paintbrushes
- Polystyrene balls

Approach

1. Show the children the Hokusai prints and discuss how the waterfalls twist and meander over the rocks like the roots of a tree.

2. Using scrunched-up tissue paper and string, recreate the twists and turns of a Hokusai waterfall. When happy with the design, glue onto a card background.

3. When dry, paint in shades of blue and sprinkle with polystyrene balls to form bubbles.

Kirifuri Falls, ca 1831, by Hokusai (1760–1849) © Christies Images/Corbis

Waterwheels

One of the first inventions to use the power of water was the waterwheel. Turned by fast-flowing rivers, they were used to drive machinery to grind corn and make cloth.

Resources
- Paints, paintbrushes and sponges
- Cartridge paper
- String
- Card and glue

Approach

1. Look at the various components of waterwheel machinery. Sketch out some designs of the machine parts.

2. On a piece of card, draw in pencil a selected machine design. Cover the pattern with string to make a printing block. Allow to dry.

3. Use a sponge to paint the background on a piece of cartridge paper. Allow to dry.

4. Paint the strings on the printing block and press it down firmly onto the painted background. Alternatively, machine parts can be drawn and painted on dyed yellow cloth.

Model Waterwheel

Approach

Resources
- Card and glue
- Dowelling
- Wood battens and saw
- Lolly sticks or spatulas
- Paints and paintbrushes
- Tubes

1. Using a compass, draw two large circles of the same size onto card. Cut them out and paint them. Pierce the centre of each circle.

2. Measure the radius of the circle. Cut eight pieces of wood to this length, then stick them down onto one circle, from the centre outwards, in a regular star shape.

3. Glue lolly sticks to the ends of the battens to make the blades.

4. Stick down the other circle, sandwiching the wood between the two circles. Push dowelling through the centre holes in the wheel.

5. Glue the tubes onto a firm piece of card, far enough apart to hold the dowelling. Cut V-shaped notches at the top of the tubes to balance the dowelling on.

Canal Art

Some rivers and streams have had their courses altered to make it easier for people to travel on them. Many canals were built as short cuts to link rivers and so speed up the transportation of goods and materials between industrial areas. Most canals are not very wide, so barges or narrow boats were used to navigate them. 'Roses and Castles' is the popular name for the traditional paintwork on narrow boats and canalware.

Resources
- Petroleum jelly
- Cellulose paste powder and water
- Scrap paper
- Paints and paintbrushes
- Coloured paper
- Pictures of 'Rose and Castle' designs
- Plastic plant pots in various sizes
- Glue

Approach

1. Cover a plant pot in a thin layer of petroleum jelly, then several layers of papier-mâché. Allow to dry.

2. Leaving the plant pot inside the papier-mâché for extra strength while decorating, paint the pot green or black. Allow to dry.

3. Look at different designs of canalware art and sketch out some ideas.

4. Cut out flowers, leaves and other decoration from brightly coloured paper. Stick them onto the papier-mâché pot.

5. Remove the pot and trim the top of the papier-mâché.

6. Add a handle and varnish if required.

Frogs and Frogspawn

Frogs live and breed in ponds and rivers. These habitats provide everything a frog needs, from the algae in the water on which they feed, to the logs and riverside holes for their winter sleep.

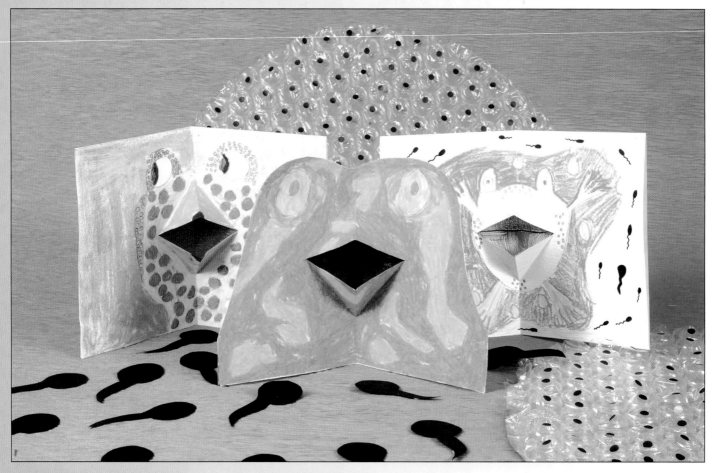

Approach

1. Cut a circle of bubble wrap and glue onto a piece of card. Dip a matchstick in black ink and make tiny dots in the middle of the raised bubbles to represent newly-laid frogs' eggs in clear jelly.

2. Fold a sheet of white paper in half. Make a 2–3cm cut through the fold. Fold the flaps outwards at an angle, then push them inwards again.

3. Open the paper and pull the flaps out to form the frog's mouth. Draw the outline of a frog's head around the mouth. Attach a backing sheet.

4. Paint the frog and display with the frogspawn as shown.

Resources
- Bubble wrap
- Card and glue
- Black ink
- Matchsticks
- White paper
- Paints and paintbrushes